NOW THAT YOU ARE
BAPTISED
LET'S TALK!

by

Reverend Angela Briscoe

Grosvenor House
Publishing Limited

This book is published by
Grosvenor House Publishing Ltd
28-30 High Street, Guildford, Surrey, GU1 3EL.
www.grosvenorhousepublishing.co.uk

A CIP record for this book
is available from the British Library

ISBN 978-1-78148-364-0

Contents

Acknowledgement

I take this opportunity to thank the Lord Jesus for saving me and keeping me in His love. I send out blessings to my dad who is always praying for me. I thank my wonderful family: Danny (my husband of thirty-six years), my daughters; Lisa, Lorraine, Danielle and Deynah; my sons-in-law, Roger and Yatish; my sisters, Patricia and Julia, for their continued support in my walk with the Lord. I give special thanks to Pastor Michael Burgher of Jesus Is Ministries Bibleway Churches UK, my daughters Lorraine and Danielle for proof reading, offering suggestions, encouragement and support in the development of this work.

Foreword

Jesus told Nicodemus, a ruler of the Jews, that in order for him to enter the kingdom of God, he needed to be born of the water and of the Spirit *(John 3:5)*. Jesus himself experienced this baptism performed by John the Baptist (Matthew 3: 13-17; Mark 1:9-11; Luke 3:21-23), and today this example from Jesus is being performed all over the world.

After attending my church for one year, I was baptised January 1999, and received the baptism of the Holy Spirit in May of that year. The water baptism experience was absolutely amazing and particularly overwhelming for me because I was baptised some years before when I was around fifteen years old. The difference, however, was that this time, I recognised I was 'saved'. In my heart I knew that I was not truly saved when I was first baptised as a teenager. Upon reflection I shiver at the thought of the reason why I was baptised at that time. It all happened because I was threatened and forced into baptism by a deacon in the church I attended with my mother. I loved Sunday school and was very keen to attend. As a result of my aptitude, I was asked to help the teacher. Excited about helping the Sunday school teacher, I looked forward to Sundays. One day, I was told that I could not help with the lessons anymore unless I was baptised. Looking back now, there was no concern whether I was actually saved, nor any talk of repentance, or if I had a desire to follow Jesus. Anyhow, I did as I was told to do and by age eighteen, I became critical about the services and frustrated with unanswered questions. The only person interested in how I felt was my earthly father.

My dad was what I call a 'closet' Christian, he believed, but attended church occasionally at special events, such as Easter services and Christmas. In our home on Sundays, most of the 'sacred' records popular with the Afro-Caribbean would be played in the house and that was the extent of his weekly worship. He was a pleasant man, and didn't really chastise me unless he was persuaded to do so by my now late mother. I was a talkative teenager and enjoyed talking to daddy. At one stage, I became so frustrated at church I told my dad that there may be something wrong with me because I was not responding the same as the other people at church whenever the Spirit of God was supposed to be moving. I felt I was such a sinner and that the Spirit of God always avoided me. I grew frustrated, and eventually left the church. Thankfully though, as time went by I realised that Jesus did not leave me and this was evident because I found myself praying at all times. Praying and reading the Bible appeared very natural to me, even though I was supposedly not 'living right'.

Living my life now as a saved person, I am of the opinion that I failed as a Christian back then because my conception into the family of God was exactly as Jesus described to Nicodemus (John 3:6 King James Version): "That which is born of the flesh is flesh; and that which is born of the Spirit is spirit." For real, I was the 'flesh' candidate. I now know that the success of our walk with God is dependent upon the conversion process. If our desire to serve God is conceived by the prompting of the Holy Spirit, then we are born of the Spirit and our life in Christ will be exciting, secure, beautiful and rewarding. On the other hand, if one is baptised because of man's persuasion only, then the walk could be subject to vulnerability and may be prone to failure, unless a spiritual conversion takes place along the way.

I thank God for a second chance and that He had never left me. I thank Him for His people who relentlessly are out there in the streets, telling unbelievers about the good news of the Gospel. I have great admiration for the many Street Pastors, and their support Prayer Warriors, who are on the streets ministering and releasing hope to the hopeless, empowering the weak and ultimately restoring lives, why?... because that was how I came to Jesus. My late pastor, Bishop C E McFarlane of the Bibleway Churches UK, approached me in the street and handed me an invitation to church. After attending for approximately one year, I surrendered my life to Christ. Yes I was truly saved, I repented and was baptised in the name of our Lord Jesus. One may ask how I came to the realisation that I was saved. I knew because I became a new person, with new perspectives, determination, values and hope.

I am passionate that newly baptised Christians are adequately supported after their baptism. The scriptures remind us that "He, who began a good work in us, is able to see it through to completion (Philippians 1:6)". However, the new Christian often have questions about their new life, and it is vitally important that this thirst for knowledge is satisfied, and they are empowered enough to stimulate their interest in seeking more of the Word of God independently. Have you ever observed a baby from about six months to ten months old? There seems to be a huge imaginary question mark in their forehead, highlighted by a frown, whenever they see a new face. Can you imagine there are lots of questions running around in their very new mind? Well, a "just born again" person could very much be in the same situation of curiosity.

As a new Christian, I asked a variety of questions too when I began my journey; many were answered when I prayed and asked God for knowledge wisdom and understanding. Others were answered by my late pastor, and I am still waiting or some answers. Nevertheless, I have a hope of glory and this knowledge comes expressly from the Word of God and I am comforted in the knowledge that The Lord is my shepherd and I shall not lack any good thing, because, if we lack, He will supply our needs according to His riches in Glory (Psalm 23, Philippians 4:19).

Pre-Baptism Notes

The following are extracts I have taken from a teaching tool I produced for ministering to believers that have expressed a desire to accept and follow the teachings of Jesus.

Many people attend church regularly, and although the Gospel is preached clearly, I still hear the question: Why be baptised? At all times, I address the question with inward excitement that they are asking because the Holy Spirit is at work, starting the 'saving' process.

If we profess we love Jesus, then why not follow the example He left us. The scriptures show how this very outward act is relevant to be saved. We read how John the Baptist baptised believers in preparation for the coming of the Kingdom of God. Also, we read how Jesus Himself asked to be baptised. If we love Him for his goodness and mercy, His care towards us, and for all the times He has been there through difficult situations, the question should then be: Why NOT be baptised?

Instruction by Jesus

Jesus expressed clearly in St John chapter 3, that we cannot see the Kingdom of God unless we are born of the water and of the Spirit. There is no uncertainty that He was serious about this instruction for us to be saved.

Being born again represents a "New Birth", all things are passed away and all things are now new. Jesus invites anyone and everyone to come to Him (Matthew 11:28-30). It clearly doesn't matter what type of life we lived before our encounter with Jesus, He does not care about our family history, or how colourful our past may have been, rather, He cares only about our heart and how we respond to Him. He wants us to have everlasting life as He had intended for us before sin came and changed the course of God's plan.

Repentance

Repentance is the first step of faith in the "New Birth" process, because forgiveness is impossible without it (Luke 13.3). You must understand that repentance is not just feelings of remorse or regret for past sins, or feeling sorry for present sins. Nor is repentance simply confessing in the hope of forgiveness (Bibleway Training Institute Theology notes). In such circumstances, a person may be prone to repeat the sins. Repentance then should be sincere and from the heart, not superficial. True repentance indicates a turn from sin to God. Yes feeling sorry is part of the process, and asking for forgiveness is important, however, the attitude toward sin after asking God to forgive your past, depicts true repentance. The Greek word for repentance is 'Metonoia', which means changing of the mind, a turn around. Basically to repent is to make a turn from your present life, views and habits and this identifies with the death of Christ on the cross. You have nailed your sins to the cross, therefore, the way you view transgressions will ultimately change.

The Water Experience

Baptism – "He that believes and is baptised shall be saved, but he that believeth not shall be dammed (Mark 16:16)." Water baptism is part of salvation. The act of going under the water (total emersion), although outwardly, is very important. It should not be looked at as simply an outward sign of an inward grace, as there is more to the experience than that sentiment. Water baptism, identifies a believer with the burial of Christ, in which the power of their sinful nature is destroyed (Bibleway Training Institute Theology notes). Obedience to Christ in this way brings a person into the family of God in the way that Jesus wants him or her to be connected. St John 15 explains that Jesus is the true vine, all other channels for example, other faiths and modern religious beliefs fundamentally appears to be man's way of trying to reach God. Jesus came to reach us, and has taught us through the scriptures that repentance, water baptism and baptism of the Holy Spirit, allows us entrance into relationship with God.

Baptism of the Holy Spirit

Jesus said God is a Spirit and we must worship Him in Spirit and truth (St John 4:24). He also expressed that we must be born of the Spirit in order for us to enter into the Kingdom of God (John 3:3-8). Therefore, part of salvation is the baptism of the Holy Spirit, where he dwells within us, and as water baptism identifies us to the burial of Christ, The Holy Spirit baptism identifies us to His resurrection.

There is no order to when the two baptisms takes place; for example, the Bible shows us clearly in Acts 10:44-46 where Cornelius and his family received the baptism of the Holy Spirit then were baptised. Jesus also encouraged us to ask for the baptism of the Holy Spirit (Luke 11:13), which indicates that this is not an automatic process.

The initial evidence of being baptised with the Holy Spirit is the speaking of tongues or language which you have not previously spoken (Acts 2:4); however, the ongoing evidence is the demonstration of the fruit of the Spirit in the life of a saved person, as featured in Galatians 5:22-23.

Jesus promised a power that will give boldness to the receiver when they are baptised with the Holy Spirit (Act 1:8), and this power is necessary for effective ministry. After discussions with some individuals about the spiritual difference between a Christian that asks God for the baptism of the Holy Spirit and receives it, as appose to the Christian that is unsure about the necessity to be baptised with the Holy Spirit. A scenario I use to explain the difference is that a powerful top of the range car, and a bottom end "run around" car, are still motor vehicles that can get you to destinations. However, the power of the engine will determine the performance in durability, speed and efficiency on the road. What car would you prefer to be available to you?

The Christian Life

Living a Christian life is wonderful. Issues which perhaps would have caused you emotional pain do not now have the same effect. Reason being that Jesus supernaturally takes away the pain and give you peace. When at times sadness is all around in your life, praying to Jesus with faith, believing that He answers prayers changes the situation. He will take the sadness and give you gladness (Psalms 45:7). I encourage you to go all the way with Jesus; the benefits are priceless.

Let's talk – When would the Change in My Life begin to Show?

This is a great question! Part of the process of change is that through His death and resurrection, Jesus Christ has applied an eraser to all the things in your life. You know, all of those experiences which perhaps you have not been very proud of. *"Therefore if any man be in Christ, he is a new creature; old things are passed away,"* erased, rubbed out! *"Behold, all things are become new* (2 Corinthians 5:17)." Spiritually you are new man, boy, girl or woman in the making. Congratulations!

Be happy in your heart, the change is a gradual process. You have done the most important part; what's that you might say? Well, it is that of confessing your sins, declaring that Christ is and will be Lord of your life, and you are now baptised. Through your response to His call and obedience to do His will, the process of a changed life has begun.

1

OK, let's look at Romans 12:2. Paul explains here that there is a renewing of the mind; he did not say an immediately renewed one. A caterpillar does not instantly change its form; there are steps to its transformation, and this is the same for a newly baptised person like you. Attitudes will become more "Christ like" over time, for example if you were once very angry or impulsive in certain circumstances, the renewed mind would apply a more peaceful approach to a negative situation, allowing the Holy Spirit to help you respond in a way that demonstrates the fruit of the Spirit (Galatians 5: 22-24). Rough edges in your life will be smoothed out as the Holy Spirit constantly scrapes away the erosions of bad habits and replaces them with new ones.

Please do not think for a minute that you should be a saint immediately. If that thought came into your mind, I encourage you to read Psalms 103; you will find this Psalm of David very comforting. Jesus knows our frame; He knows how vulnerable we are. You are precious to the Lord, Malachi 3:3 explains that He will mould you like a refiner of metal, He will never take His eyes off you. This indicates that you are like precious metal to Jesus, and precious metal takes some time to be refined. He is strong when we are weak, His strength is perfect in our weak times (2 Corinthians 12:9), take time out each day and talk to God about all your challenges. You will be fine, Jesus will be right there with you. Read Matthew 28:20, Philippians 1:6 and be encouraged that God started a good work in you and He will take you through all the stages of spiritual development.

Testimony

Some weeks after I became a Born Again Christian, I was having a meal at home around the table with my two youngest daughters. My youngest, who was then seven years old, began to shout for whatever reason, I cannot recall. At some point I got irritated with her and told her to "shut up". She immediately mumbled under her breath, so I asked what she had said. Her sister then said: "Mummy, she said that, you're baptised now so you shouldn't say 'shut up' and that the man did not dip you deep enough under the water." Well, I quickly realised that even the little children are aware that when you accept Jesus, a change should take place at some stage. I was just like you, my change was gradual as well and I'm still a work in progress.

Let's talk – What if I am Tempted to do something I used to Do?

Do not worry about this; temptation reminds us that we are children of God. Think about it, the devil does not need to tempt his own people, he has them already!

You have a weapon available to you and that is the Word of God. Learn to use God's word whenever you feel a temptation moment coming. It is great to memorize some of the Psalms of David; the words will then be in your heart and ready on your lips in every situation. Psalms 27 is one that is very helpful in difficult situations.

The enemy is very devious and tries to put obstacles in our paths. However, one thing is clear and it is that we are only tempted by our own desire. *"Let no one say when he is tempted, 'I am being tempted by God,' for God cannot be tempted by evil, and He Himself does not tempt anyone. But each one is tempted when he is carried away and enticed by his own lust* (James 1:14)."

Stumbling blocks are obstacles which can stop you in your tracks and potentially impede your progress. However, these may vary with individuals, some examples are erotic or violent television programmes and other forms of media depicting illicit dealings and improper behaviour and habits. The enemy can only operate through us if we give him space in our life. The scripture advises on dealing with the enemy in James 4:7 *"submit to God, resist the devil and he will flee."* He may try to flaunt a coloured past in your face, or he may try to confuse you or question your walk with God. Therefore, fill your heart and mind with good things; Philippians 4:8 has excellent instructions from Apostle Paul to keep your heart and mind stayed on the Lord. Be confident in the knowledge that the Lord is with you every step of the way. What works for me when I experience temptation, is to boldly say to the enemy: "Get behind me, Satan." Apostle Paul's affirmation: "I can do all things through Christ who strengthens me," is very encouraging (Philippians 4:13). Jesus will hold you up with His famous Right hand of Righteousness (Isaiah 41:10).

Temptation is an opportunity for you to make Jesus proud of your victorious achievement in conquering the enemy. It's a journey we all travel. Jesus is Lord of all the earth, and yet after He was baptised, the devil had the cheek to try and tempt the King of Kings! Imagine the cheek of it!

5

Jesus sorted him out though, and with the help of the Holy Spirit, you will sort him out too (Matthew 4: 10).

A point to remember is that temptation is not a sin, rather it is giving into the forces that create the transgression and even in this we give thanks that Jesus is faithful and just, the scripture tells us that He knows our frame (Psalms 103:14). Don't give up, there is hope! Bring all your troubles to the Lord and have the assurance that He will take care of you (Matthew 11: 28). Trust Jesus, you'll be fine. Take comfort in knowing that God is happy with the effort you make in seeking Him.

Testimony

Before I gave my heart to the Lord, I was addicted to the Bingo game. I loved Bingo so much that I did not care if I didn't win. I enjoyed the company of my fellow gamblers, and look forward to seeing them; so basically, it was like church to me, as if I was giving all my attention to this idol.

After I accepted Christ and was baptised, I lost the urge for the Bingo, because the Lord showed me that He has given me the energy to work and has provided for me. So, taking my money to gamble is demonstrating that I do not trust Him to provide all I needed. I was blown away when

I received that revelation and the encounter I had with the Lord about my habit, dissolved the lust for the bingo game.

One day my colleagues at the local Council where I worked decided to have a work social. Yes you've guessed it, at the Bingo! I tried to rationalise why it would be OK for me to go. In my head I'm thinking, it *is work that is arranging it after all.* I thought and thought, wrestled with excuses, then I looked to Jesus, I sat at my desk and spoke to the Lord. I received strength, when my memory brought me to the scripture where we read that God's strength is perfect when we are weak. At that point, I understood that this particular temptation could not be excused as an impromptu yielding, the Lord opened my eyes to the fact that I would need to complete an application form to renew a membership, which definitely would need some calculated action. Firstly, I would need to pick up a pen, enter my name and even submit the form, by getting an envelope, folding the form and handing it to the coordinator of the works social! Well, with such revelation, I rebuked the devil promptly in the name of Jesus! I then politely declined the invitation, and to God be the glory, I got the victory!

Let's talk – I don't really understand the whole "Your Body is a Temple" Thing!

This is a very common question; others have wondered about this message from Apostle Paul: "*Know you not that you are the temple of God* (1 Corinthians 3:16)?" The Holy Spirit has helped me understand what this means, and this is what I will share with you. The word says: "*Flee immorality. Every other sin that a man commits is outside the body, but the immoral man sins against his own body* (1 Corinthians 6:18)."

When Jesus left this world, he poured out His Spirit for all people, He empowers you (Joel 2:28) (Acts 2:17). The Spirit of God is now living in you, around you and at times will move upon you, for example it was the Holy Spirit that prepared your heart to accept Jesus. He connects you to Jesus, He restores joy whenever you are sad, He protects you from dangers seen and unseen, therefore it is fitting that we respect His presence because our body is the temple where He resides. With this knowledge then, there should be a conscious decision and application with regard to the treatment of your body. Would it be appropriate or respectful to go into a church, a temple or a synagogue and splash graffiti on the walls and desecrate the floors? I don't think so. God wants you to treat your body with respect and with utmost dignity, 1 Chronicles 16:9 say that God's work is wonderful. He made you marvellous; you are indeed a wonderful creation. This awesome reality should usher a believer into respecting the human temple of God here on earth, which is our body.

There are lots of benefits to this beautiful concept of keeping the body holy, such as better health, as you would be more mindful of what goes into your body by way of food; your lungs will benefit because there would be a heightened sense of the need not to fill them with harmful pollutants; your views on sexual immorality would start to change. The bible warns that sex outside of God's will (fornication) can have damaging effects spiritually, as it negatively impacts on our relationship with God (Colossians 3:5). If we continue to be mindful that our body is the temple of God on earth, this will ultimately promote morally healthy minds and a deep relationship with Jesus our Lord. The Word of God will help in areas where you may be struggling. The Holy Bible tells us: *"The Lord is righteous in all his ways and holy in all His works. The Lord is nigh (near) unto all them that call upon Him in truth. He will fulfil the desire of them that fear*

Him. Our heavenly father also will hear their cry, and will save them. The LORD preserves all them that love Him (Psalm 145:17-21)." How awesome is that!

The revelation of how important your body as the earthly temple of Christ actually is, will ultimately come from the Lord, so be comforted, He will reveal His truths to you as you read and get deeper in His Word. Society legislates that one can do whatever they desire with regard to their body in giving themselves to another, after the age of sixteen. However, those who are in Christ Jesus are required to be set apart from the world. 1 Peter 2:9 says: "*But ye are a elect race, a royal priesthood, a holy nation, a people for 'God's' own possession, that ye may show forth the excellences of Him who called you out of darkness into his marvellous light.*" God knows what we need before we ask. It was our Lord who decided that it was not good for Adam to be alone and created his soul mate Eve (Genesis 2:18). He will take care of your physical needs, when you, are ready. You'll be fine.

Let's talk – Do I have to attend Church all the time?

You are the church; all the people make up the church, so if you are not there, it's like a little piece of the family of God is missing in your assembly. In my experience, one of the main reasons for irregular attendance to church services is the individual not yet realising their purpose in God. Ask Jesus to show you the ministry He has for you, because the Scripture is very clear that He has a plan to prosper you. (Jeremiah 29:11-13).

There will be times you cannot physically be at church and taking time out to meditate and be alone with God is necessary at times. However, it would not be spiritually healthy if you were to stay at home for weeks upon weeks, as there could be a danger of losing focus.

Recently people are enjoying services at home. Modern technology enables national and international Christian preachers from many countries to minister to people in their homes. Believers can also enjoy seminars on the internet via podcasts. This is probably fine for Christians who are housebound due to mobility restrictions, however, Paul encourages us to be sure not to forsake the coming together of ourselves (Hebrews 10:25).

There are so many benefits to collective worship, just like a weekend meal where all the family engages in lively discussions around the dining table, similarly, in church you engage in lively praise and worship, and benefit from hearing motivating testimonies from other brethren. Consistent attendance at collective worship enables you to realise that you are not alone in any given situation. You are not isolated in your challenges. It could be that the blessings you enjoyed during the week and perhaps had not actually recognised as blessings become apparent to you after hearing the testimonies of others. Another excellent benefit of collective worship is the participation in kingdom building activities, which promotes spiritual growth. It is great for new converts to share their skills to advance the kingdom of God, try your very best not to miss out.

An important point to note also is that God the Creator gave us Monday to Friday for work. If we are employed, we arrive at work on time and usually leave seven hours after the start time. For those who worship on a Saturday or Sunday, service may be approximately one to two hours long; some assemblies also hold evening service. Now consider this, God has faithfully and generously provided us with enough days to earn what we need to live comfortably. Is it such a chore then, to allocate a few hours to worship Him in the presence of fellow worshipers? Fellowship makes the praises to God glorious; therefore, I encourage you to endeavour to maximise your spiritual growth potential. If you should conduct a survey, you will find that many ministers would be of the opinion that regular attendance to church services is a glorious activity for strengthening your faith. David beautifully expressed his feelings on the coming together of the church: "*Behold, how good and how pleasant it is for brethren to dwell together in unity* (Psalms 133:1)." If you struggle in this area, ask God to strengthen your steps and make you steadfast in appreciating the awesomeness of collective worship. You will be fine!

Testimony

You need to be aware of potential hindrances when you are a new Christian. The enemy sometimes may appear in the guise as acquaintances and may try to distract you from attending church services. One member of the church I pastor testified that:

A friend who helped her with general repairs around the house, always seem to turn up on Sundays just when she was preparing to leave for church. Although she made it very clear that she had to be in church a particular time, he was never in a hurry to leave. He would have a drink, take a seat and begin talking about all sorts. She invited him to attend church with her, but he had many excuses. She encouraged him to seek Jesus because he had been dealing with some health issues for several months which had become worse, and had appeared depressed on occasions. She took time to listen to his concerns regarding his health, and again would encourage him to seek Jesus. She bought him a bible, which he accepted, however, said his wife is not interested in God therefore, he could not let her see him reading it.

The impromptu turning up at the house on Sundays went on over several months until after reading the Word of God, and having listened to several messages about being mindful about the strategies of the enemy, she realised that her friend unwittingly was being used as a distraction and a stumbling block to her spiritual growth. She told him that she was happy for him to visit on other days; however, he should not come on a Sunday because that was her day for collective worship. She became passionate about Christian fellowship and is now wiser as to different types of distractions that have the potential to hinder her progress in Christ.

You need to realise that the devil does not care about you, he basically want to block the blessing Christ has purposed for you at the service. Likewise, you also can be a distraction to yourself, by falling prey to vain excuses such as, *I have to get ready for work the next day; I have to clean my car; Sunday is the only time I get to do my laundry; I am all nasal and feel a cold coming on*. These are all real excuses I have heard in my role as pastor.

Suggestion

Be encouraged to develop a prayer life where you can be intimate with the Lord, then Jesus will reveal the purpose and the plans He has for you in the advancement of the Kingdom of God. When you focus and digest the Word, a Godly passion would prompt you to want to attend services regularly and the need to share the Gospel of Jesus would become evident to fellow brethren as well as those who are unchurched. Have a discussion with the department leaders; tell them about skills and achievements you may have, which could be helpful in church activities—get involved. You will be fine!

Let's talk – I'm not sure if I should let my friends and colleagues know that I am a born again Christian.

This is an area which affects quite a lot of Christians, not that they are ashamed of their faith, but it is the pressures of "political correctness" placed upon them by society that makes it so difficult for some people to share their belief, especially in a work environment. This is very much like the Babylonian system of the Old Testament when King Nebuchadnezzar, sanctioned a rule and made a public execution threat to anyone caught praying to the God of Israel (Daniel 6:1-28). Like Daniel, we need to stand up for Jesus. The lions' den may not be a literal one in this time, however, persecutions from a "politically correct" stand point seems similar in my view. Nevertheless, in this, we must be strong and be proud that our faith is all about love.

Society is happy to hear that love is needed and would embrace this notion in a medium such as the Beatles' song

All You Need is Love, da, da, da, da, da, but deny the author of love, which is Jesus Christ! You will need to make a decision to let them know your faith, you may then be surprised how well this is received, and even more surprised when you discover there are more Christians working in your company than you may have thought. There are companies with active Christian Union organisations, which allow staff workers the opportunity to meet during the working week.

Jesus said: "You are the light of the world (Matthew 5:14-15)." Individually, we are the light in our environment, and collectively we are the light in the world. Therefore, being bold and declaring your faith is a wonderful step towards standing up for Jesus.

The Holy Bible tells us of a man named Nicodemus, who went to see Jesus in the night, indicating that he did not want his colleagues to know his faith (St John 3). Some may argue that he had valid reasons because of his political standing, however, Luke 9:26 give us an idea of our position with God if we should be ashamed of Him. Pray and ask God how you should approach every situation concerning Him, He will make you courageous; He will strengthen your heart.

There are many people that are unchurched and sharing your faith could make such a positive difference to non-believers. Some people you meet may have never read the Bible, yet want to know about Jesus. In such cases, you are what they will read about the Gospel of Christ. Many unbelievers look to the Christian's lifestyle before reading the Holy Bible. The scripture tells us that after Jesus raised Lazarus from the dead, there was a banquet. Many people attended the party, not only because Jesus the great healer and messiah was there, rather, they wanted to see Lazarus; their interest was in the miracle (John 12:9). Be bold and declare your faith, you will be blessed awesomely and abundantly, because your new life in Christ is like a miracle. You'll be fine.

Testimony

I always felt confident letting my colleagues know that I am Born Again, however, they seldom engaged in conversation about my faith. I became active in the Christian Union and my managers knew that one day a week I would attend the meetings. One day I had a call from a manager who had been off sick for some time; she wanted to speak to the Head of department, but before she ended the conversation with me, she told me that she needed me to pray for her. I was taken aback, but quickly said, "Yes I will definitely pray."

There may be a time in everyone's life when they have a spiritual need to reach out to God. The assurance of His promise of everlasting life is available for all. Therefore, "born again" Christians should be mindful of the responsibility they have to bring others to the knowledge of Jesus Christ.

Let's Talk – I don't know much about the Bible yet: How do I explain My Faith?

You are not expected to know the whole Bible by heart; however, you do need to know about your faith. It is important to know who God is, who Christ is and who you are in Christ, and have knowledge of who the Holy Spirit is in the world and in your life.

The Bible consists of sixty-six books divided into two parts, the Old and New Testaments. Both sections work together, for example, the Word contained in the Old Testament is explained in the New. Timothy chapter 2:15 explains that we should study to show ourselves approved. Basically, a Christian needs to know that God is the Creator of the world and all that exists was made by Him, and that God is a Spirit (St John 4:24).

Jesus, the promised Messiah of the Old Testament is the physical manifestation of God in the New Testament, He is

Emanuel meaning God with us (Isaiah 9:6-7, John 1:1, John 1:14). Jesus sacrificed himself on Calvary's cross to secure our salvation; however, in order to inherit eternal life, we need to make him Lord of our life here in the land of the living, by following His precepts.

The Holy Spirit is the Spirit of God, released in the world and in the lives of people. The purpose of the Holy Spirit is to be a comforter and a guide for the people of God, until His work on Earth is finished (John 14:16).

Knowing who you are in Christ is very important because this knowledge will help you understand your purpose. There are many examples throughout the Bible which will help awaken your awareness of who you are in God.

- ✓ *You are accepted* (Ephesians 1:6)
- ✓ *You are a child of God* (John 1:12)
- ✓ *You are joint heir with Jesus* (Romans 8:1)
- ✓ *You are chosen of God* (Colossians 3:12)
- ✓ 1 John 3:3 explains that you are loved

How awesome is it, that we are so special to God. Your knowledge will increase as you seek to know more of Jesus. You'll be fine!

Let's talk – I've met many Unfriendly People that goes to Church: How do I deal with this?

I love this question because I have had to explain this to so many people in my role as a minister. Firstly, always remember, we are 'people' and some of us unfortunately behave unseemly at times; however, in most situations, people are not unfriendly without a reason. John 3:16 says that God loves us so much, He sent His son to die for our sins, and this is a starting point to understanding difficult characters. You see, irrespective of what we do, He loves us; we need to then extend this love to others because we are all His children, even if at times we don't behave like it.

As a minister, there have been occasions where complaints have been brought to me about the attitude of some individuals. At a point in the complainant's passion when expressing their concerns, I would often hear "... *and she or he is supposed to be a Christian.*" My response is to make them realise that, yes, they are, Christians! There may be several children in a family, and no doubt their characters will be different. If one behaves badly, that behaviour does not change their parentage; therefore, God is still father to the person that has caused the upset. The strategy to help hurting people is to show love and care, engage them in conversation, and if this is welcomed, lead them into prayer for healing and deliverance.

The children at the church I attend performed a play written by the Sunday school teacher. The play was called 'The Christmas Gringe'. This character attended church regularly, most of the time she was pleasant, but at Christmas, she became very angry and impatient with everyone at church. The lady did not want the pastor to agree the Nativity play for the children, which made them very sad. The 'Gringe' would disturb practice times and hinder their progress. One little girl decided to talk to the lady. She asked her why she was always so angry, and that she would love to see her happy. The little girl was surprised because the lady began to cry, and explained that a very sad event which tore her family apart, took place around Christmas time many years before. They prayed together and because of the caring attitude of the little girl, the hurting lady realised that her pain was causing others pain. She changed her attitude from that day. Although this was fiction for the Christmas play, there are people experiencing inward pain, which unfortunately comes out in their behaviour.

Many people have issues and forget that being in a church fellowship is the right environment for healing and deliverance. "*Now a certain man was there who had an infirmity thirty-eight years. When Jesus saw him lying there, and knew that he already had been in that condition a long time, He said to him, 'Do you want to be made well (St John 5:6)?'*" We need to remember that like this man, who waited so long for his healing, although he was essentially in the right place, there are many people in churches waiting for that helping hand in achieving their deliverance and healing.

As you grow in the Lord, you will find that the church is like a hospital, and it will take a little time for some people to recover from their spiritual ailments. 1 Peter 3:8 says we are to show love to our brethren and be mindful of their feelings. Psalms 119:165 says you will have great peace when you serve the Lord and you will never be offended. I encourage you to be like the little girl who cared enough to speak to the lady they called 'the Gringe' and you'll be fine.

Let's talk – Would it be a Problem to Date someone who is Not a Christian?

This is a question that has been raised over and over again. It is also a question that the Holy Scriptures points out beautifully; *"... don't be unequally yoked with unbelievers, for what fellowships have righteousness and iniquity* (2 Corinthians 6:14)?" Paul is not saying that we are to drop our friends who have not yet accepted the Gospel; rather, he is addressing the question of intimate relationships, which could potentially lead to marriage.

We are living in a permissive society, where there is more sexual freedom and a non-believer may find it difficult to understand the importance of honouring one's body. They may want more from the relationship and if you are serious about your faith, you will not want to deliver. The Word of God explains clearly, *"... the natural man cannot understand the things of God because they are spiritually discerned* (1 Corinthians 2: 14)."

We as human beings are anxious, and want everything quickly, therefore we panic about such things as finding a wife or a husband, and we sometimes behave as if it is a crisis in our life, having passed certain age. The reason for this panic could be a result of our inability to view God's provision in the long term. Try not to panic, Jesus will take care of your needs and good desires of your heart. The scripture says, "*Do not be anxious about anything, but in everything, by prayer and petition, with thanksgiving, present your requests to God* (Philippians 4:6)."

Ultimately, it is your decision to go on a date with a non-Christian but yes to your question, this could present some problems, with regard to expectations. A situation could arise where pressure could be placed upon you, which could potentially impact negatively on your walk with God.

If in the event you should meet someone you are attracted to and they are not "born again", be bold and shine your light, invite them to your place of worship. God knows the plan he has for you (Jeremiah 29: 11-14), likewise He knows the plan he has for the person too. Should your friend accept Jesus as his or her personal Saviour and a relationship towards each other grow seriously, then I encourage you to allow Jesus to be the centre of that relationship. It is important to develop a regular prayer time with each other also. Whenever possible, plan dates with mutual Christian friends, grow in the Lord, and ask The Lord for wisdom to make Godly decisions (Proverbs 3:7). Proverbs 3:5 advises beautifully, that we should not rely on our own understanding, so I am of the opinion that in all aspects of the relationship, you should endeavour to put God first, make Him your counsellor, ask for guidance and He will help you in all you do. You'll be fine!

Let's talk – Is there a Right or Wrong way to Dress: Why is there such an Issue about Clothes?

Unfortunately, there may always be an issue with clothes when it comes to church, because people have varying views on 'modesty' (1Timothy 2:9). I am of the view that unsaved women in the days of Timothy dressed elaborately, therefore, his instruction perhaps was relating to expensive clothing, rather than revealing garments. It was a time that the churches were being established and there were many poor and needy people, a Christian woman being adorned in costly outfits could perhaps be seen as insensitive to the more important needs of the less financially able.

For many years, women have been and largely still a target for criticism against their sense of dress in a worship setting; more recently, men have been a focus due to ill-fitting trousers and tight shirts. I believe that educating people about appropriate dress whatever the environment should be of more importance, than allowing our brothers and sisters to feel their garment is a sin against God, when in reality our dress sense is not essential to salvation.

Dress code in formal worship during the Old Testament time was very important in a priestly capacity. We see this in 1 Samuel 30:7-8 when King David wanted guidance from God to retrieve that which was stolen from him. Before praying he asked the High Priest to bring him his ephod which was a stately apron-like gown with beautiful ornaments and rich embroidery commonly used among the High Priest, when seeking the Lord. This gives an insight into David's attitude towards how he should present himself in the presence of God. Robing in this manor is still practiced in churches today depending on the formality of the occasion. Fortunately though, unless you are of high office, you don't have to worry about robes. However, it does demonstrate that there is an element of order in the presence of the Lord, which reveals a profound sense of appropriateness, and it would be wonderful if all Christians take ownership of this.

After discussions with a group of young people, the general consensus was that inappropriate clothing, especially when one is ministering, could be a distraction for fellow brethren, and may negatively affect the focus on worship. For example, it could be very distracting to have someone stand at the pulpit ministering and areas of their body are spilling out, or garments so tight that parts of the anatomy are clearly defined. The Bible says *God looks at the heart, and man look at the outward appearance* (1 Samuel 16:7), therefore as mere mortals, only seeing the outward, it is wise to make the outward less of a distraction to others in an environment where all focus should be on Jesus.

In my opinion, there is no wrong or right way to dress for church, rather the focus should be on the suitability. Common sense should prompt you to dress sensibly for the occasion; for example, at the office, jeans, track suits and trainers would be deemed unprofessional attire unless it's a 'charity event' where staff would dress down, to raise money. A uniform identifies an officer and so on. Dress also dictates status and authority, so for me, an awareness of appropriate and relevant attire is key to eliminate dress sense issues.

A 'born again' Christian, would be guided by the Holy Spirit with regard to dress sense in the house of the Lord, as well as on the street, literally anywhere you go, because you are the light of the world and ought to be ready for ministry at all times (St Matthew 5 v14). However, there are situations, when it does not need the Holy Spirit to tell you that basically, you are uncomfortable due to what you are wearing. Therefore, whether you are at church, in a shopping centre, or on the street, and feel the need to constantly pull down a skirt, or fix a blouse, or in the case of a man, constantly adjusting your posture due to tight fitting trousers, science and logic will tell you that the outfit is not practical.

Remember though, change is gradual. Take one step at a time, and you will get there. Be assured that you have amazing support in Jesus. He will prompt you and tell you when that outfit perhaps should stay in the wardrobe. God will keep you and strengthen you with His famous right hand, so have no fear (Isaiah 41:10). You'll be fine!

Let's talk – I Love Music: Can I still listen to my Secular Music?

Music is wonderful, it gives us joy, but it is also an intrusive force and does not ask your permission to enter your head. Once music comes to your hearing, it may remain in your subconscious and often manifests (show) hours after you had first heard the tune. It does this in a way that you may spontaneously burst into song or humming, and may leave you pondering, "Where did I hear that tune?" Music is beautiful and can be spiritually profound. It is a wonderful opening in the act of praise and worship. Music is universal, God-given and should be appreciated. Skill and intellect is required to write and perform music, and this blessing, could only be bestowed upon individuals by our Heavenly Father.

King David, who is one of the main contributors to the Psalms, loved music and had an outstanding orchestra. With his skilful mastery on the harp, he calmed a troubled King Saul, the first King of Israel (1 Samuel 16:23). Beethoven the great composer wrote nine symphonies and many more musical works and he was just one of many who received such blessings from the Lord. In relatively modern times we have had great musicians from all walks of life, blessed with the skill and talent to produce wonderful music and songs. History has shown us gifted people throughout the ages with amazing testimonies that have written profound hymns that will continuously bring joy to generations.

The question perhaps should be whether it is appropriate to listen to secular lyrics rather than secular music, because some secular lyrics are extremely inappropriate in general. The inappropriateness is largely due to bad language and explicit sexual connotations, which is not conducive to people who are endeavouring to live in the will of God. For example, some secular songs glamourize a lifestyle that glorifies the devil, in that it may promote violence, and gender inequality and disrespect. The Word of God tells us that we should, "Let no corrupt communication proceed out of our mouth (Ephesians 4:29)." Apostle Paul encourages us to sing spiritual songs and psalms with gratitude to God (Colossians 3: 16).

Essentially, it is your choice as to what music or songs you listen to, so pray and ask the Lord to renew your mind and lead you in the path of righteousness (Psalms 23 :3). You will be fine because as you develop in your walk with God, the Holy Spirit will guide you in making the right decisions. If you make a bad choice along the way, just look at it as a learning exercise, and Jesus will help you get it right.

Let's talk – I'm told it is best to read my Bible every day: But is that Realistic?

It would be great, absolutely great to read the Word of God meaningfully every day. For some people this is realistic with the discipline of morning devotions, using tools like "The Word for Today", a monthly devotion booklet and other Bible study literature.

Many years ago when I attended Sunday school, there was a song we sang to encourage the importance of reading the Bible: "Read your Bible, pray every day, pray every day, if you want to grow." The lyrics sings out the reason why the Word of God is best read on a daily basis, this promotes spiritual growth. Just as we need food for our body, we need God's Word. Think about this: if you don't eat for several days, your strength suffers, vital systems starts shutting down, danger of malnutrition becomes apparent. The Word of God is food to a believer's soul— spiritual food for life.

The Word is alive and speaks to your very being. One can read a novel or a magazine and may get some pleasure in reading it. The Bible on the other hand is vastly different because Jesus communicates with you through the Scriptures. 2 Timothy 3:16 explains why sometimes you would open the Holy Bible and be led to text or a body of Scripture that speaks to your situation at that time. The Word navigates your walk with Christ.

Sitting down with the open pages everyday may not be realistic for everyone. However, our God is so great, He has anticipated our busy schedules and through modern technology, He inspired a Bible application, which is available on the mobile phone! Think about it, you are living in an "on the go" society and with the Word of God available at a touch of a button, or the slide of your finger, the Bible can be read anywhere outside the home. Basically, we don't have any excuse.

The habit of reading the Word often is an excellent way to stay connected to Jesus. When you pray, you are talking to God, expressing your desires and needs. An important point to remember is that whenever you read the Word, Jesus speaks to *you*. New babe, please do not be overwhelmed, just think of the Bible as your journey planner.

NOW THAT YOU ARE BAPTISED LET'S TALK!

I would encourage you to read this instruction from the Lord: *This book of the law shall not depart from your mouth, but you shall meditate on it day and night, so that you may be careful to do according to all that is written in it; for then you will make your way prosperous, and then you will have success. "Have I not commanded you? Be strong and courageous! Do not tremble or be dismayed, for the LORD your God is with you wherever you go* (Joshua 1:1-9)." Whatever biblical translation you read this passage of scripture from, it is very clear that God wants us to meditate on His words.

Testimony

My second daughter left home for university, and before she travelled, her aunt (my sister) gave her a little gift box. My daughter opened the box to reveal a Bible, which was beautifully bound with a zip. As she was in a hurry to catch a coach, she quickly closed the box and said her goodbyes. Approximately three weeks later, my daughter called from university; she was excited as she explained that she decided to read her Bible, which was still packed away. When she opened it, folds of money fell out. My sister said she was waiting to see how long it would take before the Bible was opened. Overall, she was impressed that her niece decided to read the Bible within a month of leaving home for university.

My sister gave her niece more than money that day, because my daughter realised that there are also heavenly treasures in the Bible. After leaving university she gave her heart to the Lord and is strong in her faith today.

Let's talk – I know People who are Atheist: Now that I'm a Christian, how should I React to Them?

The first thing we must understand is our purpose as Christians. What is your 'job description'? This role is revealed in (St Matthew 22: 39). Every person who claims that they are an atheist, have a heart that Jesus can mould. We just have to allow them the opportunity to hear Jesus through us.

The Christian's job is to love. The condition of the people is not for us to judge, that is Jesus' job. If a person is living outside the will of God, then the Holy Spirit's job is to convict (make them realise). St John 3:16 says that God sent His only Son that whosoever believes in Him. The emphasis then is on 'whomever', which indicates that there are going to be non-believers. We should not presume that anyone is beyond saving, as in the days of Jonah, who judged the people of Nineveh as beyond saving.

St Mathew 7:1 clearly says we should not judge others, or we ourselves will be subjected to being judged. We do not know the heart of people; they may have a secret relationship going on as in the account of Nicodemus' secret visits to learn from Jesus (St John 3:1). When we love, the grace of God is seen in us, and when the "love they neighbour" process takes place a change in the opposing individual is inevitable. An example can be found in the account of Zacchaeus, a Tax Collector, who was judged as beyond saving by his local community, but loved by Jesus (Luke: 19). When we love, Jesus makes the change happen. Therefore, my answer to this question is to react with love. There is a phrase that says, "Don't hate the player hate the game (Love the person, hate the action)."

As a born again person I am of the persuasion that our actions can bring any non-believer to Christ. Most people do not have the horrifying reputation that Apostle Paul had before his conversion. Acts 9, will tell you about his amazing conversion, Paul was what many today would call an extremist. Yet Jesus was able to use Paul's passion and commitment for the advancement of the Kingdom of God! Strive to celebrate your love for Jesus by sharing His Gospel to all who cares to listen, and pray for those who are not interested. You'll be fine.

Testimony

One day I attended a Christian Union (CU) gathering at my place of work. The CU had invited a local church community group to do a presentation as they had started an initiative, by going into schools to talk to teenagers about Jesus. In order to do this, they needed a sponsor within the school. A particular school had a very successful workshop and continuously invited the group back. The sponsor that had made it possible for the Christian group to visit the school was a teacher who claimed to be an atheist! Many young people accepted the Lord as a result.

This experience taught me that we can never presume to know the condition of a person's heart. Our passion should be a commitment to talk of Jesus to all, and then they can decide if they want to listen.

Let's talk – I hear about Fasting: Do I have to Fast Regularly?

Fasting has purpose, and there are three main reasons why we enter into fasting. People fast for either spiritual, physical (cosmetic) and medically related reasons. To answer your question, fasting regularly is a matter of choice, not a rule.

Fasting is scriptural and is an excellent discipline for spiritual growth, especially when linked with prayer. Philippians 4:6 says that we should *be careful for nothing; but in everything by prayer and supplication with thanksgiving let your requests be made known unto God.* Paul did not outline fasting in this instruction; therefore, I am of the opinion that it is a personal desire. The important thing though, is that fasting has to be entered into with the right motive. If you simply want to lose weight, then go on a diet and you will get a favourable result. If you want to get closer to God, then you need to do a fast accompanied with prayer.

Jesus approves of fasting and also instructed us not to make a show when we are fasting. "*Whenever you fast, do not put on a gloomy face as the hypocrites do, for they neglect their appearance so that they will be noticed by men when they are fasting. Truly I say to you, they have their reward in full. But you, when you fast, anoint your head and wash your face so that your fasting will not be noticed by men, but by your Father who is in secret; and your Father who sees what is done in secret will reward you* (St Matthew 6 : 16-18)."

Encourage yourself to fast whenever possible and try to pray regularly throughout the fasting. God will renew your strength as promised in Isaiah 40:31. There are benefits when you enter into the right fast that of seeking the face of God. The experience will bring you into total submission where you are renewed in mind, body and soul. There may be things going on in your life which are stunting your progress then suddenly you get this Divine urge to fast, even the number of fasting days may come to you. If you are blessed with this opportunity, just be obedient, because your breakthrough could be at the end of that fast.

If your church decides to call a 'whole church' fast, please try your very best to participate, with your whole heart. This type of collective fast can restore individuals, families, churches, communities and nations. Queen Esther of the

Old Testament called a very significant three days fast, which allowed her to receive favour to the saving of a nation (Esther 4:16). You'll be fine.

Testimony

A point to note is that there are other fasting activities you can do, which do not necessarily relate to food.

Some years ago we decided to have a television fast for one week. The plan was that the television would not be turned on and that only gospel music would be played throughout our home. My husband was an avid television viewer, and the alternative did not seem exciting for him, because he was not a practicing Christian. The children and I attended church regularly and he would accompany us periodically. Nevertheless he was honourable and braved the television fast.

By middle of the week, the fast was going really well because we all adjusted to listening to the radio only, which was very calming. We prayed and read the Bible together. My husband began humming and singing the gospel songs, to the extent that he bought compact discs for his car. which he listened to whilst driving to work. The fasting was a success and in the process, my husband gave his heart to Jesus and was later baptised!

44

Let's talk – I don't fully understand the Spirit and Flesh War

In situations where you need to do something God has instructed, whether it is from the Word directly, or perhaps just lending a hand to someone in need, the flesh appears quite practical and plausible with reasons why you should not obey. For example, God told Moses that he should go to Egypt to free His people. Moses knew that this would take some kind of talking and presentation skill, so the flesh jumped up with quite a plausible excuse and said, "But I stammer so cannot speak (Exodus 4:10)." You need to understand that God is all powerful, so if He is giving you an instruction, any flesh deficiency you may have, will never be a hindrance to the task.

A classic example of the spirit and flesh at war is in the ministry of giving. 2 Chronicles 29:31 reminds us that we should bring an offering into church for the work of the Lord: "Then *Hezekiah answered and said, 'Now ye have consecrated yourselves unto Jehovah; come near and bring sacrifices and thank-offerings.'"* In such a situation, the flesh would remind you that you have other bills to deal with and yet you are thinking of church offering. On the other hand, the Spirit will remind you that when you give with a willing heart, the Lord promised to open the windows of heaven and pour out a blessing on your life (Malachi 3:10). Obedience to the Spirit of God will always have long-term benefits. David said we should bless the Lord and forget not His benefits (Psalms 103:2).

Jesus explains in St John Chapter 3 that, to be born of the flesh is flesh, and that which is born of the Spirit is Spirit. We are human beings, therefore our first reaction would be in the flesh and so everything we do is firstly centred on us, our desires, our achievements, our aims, our objectives, which most often has unhappy results. A born again Christian would be inclined to avoid the urges of the flesh, because they have accepted Christ in their heart and the Holy Spirit will now be their guide. Galatians 5:19-21 gives a clear outline of the works of the flesh.

Everything about the Spirit is focused on the things of God which ultimately promotes a favourable outcome in every situation. The fruit of the Spirit are listed in Galatians 5:22 and it is preferable that they should be observed in order to overcome the ways of the flesh. The scripture encourages that we should walk in the Spirit and in doing so we would not carry out the lust of the flesh. How do we walk in the Spirit then?

Here are three scenarios with a 'flesh' and 'Spirit' reaction

1. Violet attending a community meeting, Sue a fellow committee member who lived fairly close to Violet's home, also attended. At the end of the meeting, Violet asked Sue for a lift home as her car was with the mechanics.

Nope, sorry, I'm not going your way! (She thinks my car runs on water!)

Flesh

Oh sorry, Violet, I'm not going your way today, but I can drop you to a bus stop. Which bus stop will be good for you? (Oh I do hope she will be OK.)

Spirit

2. Mary needs to meet Margaret and John. She missed her train and is unable to phone because she is now out of phone credit.

John (Flesh) – *That girl she is so out of order, look how long we've been waiting. I'm so annoyed with her; she is always doing this. I should just go home, that will teach her!*

Margaret (Spirit) – *It's OK, John, she must be anxious too, I'll pray that she is OK; remember she is coming a long way to meet us. Don't worry, everything will be fine.*

3. Reverend Smith is new in the local church. One day he met his grown-up daughter at the train station. His parishioners have not met his daughter yet. At the station, a member of his congregation spotted him greeting her.

   Flesh – OMG pastor is having an affair, I better hide, can't let him see me. OMG can't wait to tell sister Rose, I'll text her now! OMG, I wonder, how long it's been going on!

   Spirit – "Oh there is pastor, I must go over. Hello, pastor, good to see you."

   Pastor – "Oh, Brother Paul, good to see you, meet my daughter, she lives in Wales and is spending the weekend with us."

The fruit of the Spirit is: love, joy, peace, longsuffering, gentleness, goodness, faith, meekness, and temperance, and you can see that no fruit of the spirt was demonstrated in the 'flesh' responses. The Lord wants us to walk in the Spirit and receive favour from Him. Take a moment and look back at some past conversations you may have had with negative or positive results, then reflect on what fruit was applied.

Prayer Suggestions

Jesus instructs us in (St John 15:1 – 10) that we should stay connected to him because He is the True Vine. This instruction to 'Abide' was repeated nine times from the fourth verse through to the tenth. It begs then to understand that our Heavenly Father really wants us to, without a doubt, remain connected, and I believe that prayer is the key factor to this request. Helen Steiner-Rice the poet penned the ode, "*Prayer is the stair we must climb every day. If we mean to see God, there is no other way.*" A Christian life then, is to constantly walk and talk with Jesus.

Jesus' disciples asked Him to teach them how to pray (Luke 11 v 1). We are also reminded in (Luke 18 v1) that men should always pray and not to lose heart, basically not to give up on hope.

A newly baptised person may also ask, how do I pray? I have heard some say: "I cannot pray like the people at church, I can never be as good as that." I encourage you please;

do not feel that you need to pray like the next person. Jesus tells us that when we pray, we are not to use vain repetitions, because we will not be heard for our many words (St Matthew 6: 7).

Praying essentially is having a conversation with God, therefore it should be a dialogue not a monologue. It is good to pause at moments during prayer, ask the Holy Spirit to assist you, wait for a moment until you feel there is a connection, stop, listen and Jesus will speak to you. In my prayer life, I use the following five steps, I treat this as my 'a b c' to prayer. I hope they can be useful to you in developing your own effective way to stay connected to the True Vine.

Guide to Prayer

1) *Greet God by honouring His Holy Name.*

2) *Spend time in worship by acknowledging and appreciating His mighty works in the world around you, and in your life.*

3) *Give Him thanks for His mercies because they are new every day. Thank Him for His faithfulness in keeping you through the night, because when you are asleep, you are vulnerable. Thank Him for his loving kindness in giving you a new day in which you can be with your family, in which you can work,*

worship and acknowledge that you are blessed with the opportunity to tell Him how much you love Him. Give Him thanks because He has released the Holy Spirit into the world and into your life.

4) *Repent of sins. We may feel that we've not done anything wrong since our last prayer, however, (Psalms 19:12) reminds us that we may be unaware of iniquities such as the type David refers to as 'secret faults.' For these we must also ask for forgiveness. Release forgiveness on those who have offended you.*

At this point, you have passed the gates of praise and worship; you have offered thanks and sought repentance. Focus on the Lord now. If other matters flash in your mind, immediately ask the Holy Spirit to centre your mind on Jesus. Ignore noises in your surroundings that may cause you to lose focus. Stay in the moment, enter in and talk to the Lord in the inner courts of prayer. Jesus assures us that if you ask it shall be given, if you seek you shall find, knock and it shall be open to you. Go ahead and ask.

New babe in Christ, a point to observe in all your talking to God, is to trust Him to work things out for you. Bring to Him all your cares and concerns. Be comforted that He will be there for you. Some years ago, I came upon a poem which helped me tremendously. The author is unknown, but whoever the person is, I thank God for them.

As children bring their broken toys in tears for us to mend,

So we bring our dreams to God because He is our friend,

But instead of leaving him in peace to work it out alone,

We hang around and try to help in ways that is our own.

Alas! We cry, my God why are you so slow?

My child He says, what could I do?

You never did let go.

The poem speaks for itself. God is Almighty, so *he is able to do exceedingly abundantly, more than you ask or think* (Ephesians 3: 20-21). When you bring your issues to Him, I encourage you to wait and trust that He will answer your prayers. There is a benefit to waiting for God to do things in His time. Isaiah says: "*But they that wait upon the LORD shall renew their strength; they shall mount up with wings as eagles; they shall run, and not be weary; and they shall walk and not faint* (Isaiah 40:31)."

God does not need our assistance to fulfil the promises He has made to us. Timing is important to God and He will always show up because the scriptures tell us that *He is our present help in times of trouble* (Psalms 46:1). You do not know your tomorrow, because there is no guarantee of tomorrow, we know of the concept, and so we make our plans, but actually, we only have today. He sees what we cannot see, because He is all knowing, therefore, His blessings, deliverance, healing and all breakthroughs will come when you are ready in your heart to receive them. Let go and let God, you'll be fine!

Testimonies

A selection of testimonies relating to some of the featured questions:

Instant change of a habit

About September 2000, not long after I was truly saved, I met a beautiful lady who was from a Muslim background, but had desired to know Jesus. After discussions with her, I learned that this desire to know the Lord began years before we met. She is now late, and her name was Rosa. After ministering to her, she accepted Jesus, and in fact was one of those people privileged to be baptised with the Holy Spirit before her water baptism the following year.

One Sunday, Rosa testified at church that, she had been smoking from her early teens. On the day of her baptism, she had a strong urge to smoke. She decided, "OK, this will be my last cigarette." She explained that she went into her garden, lit the cigarette, and then proceeded to take a draw. As she took that draw, a vile taste came into her mouth, she immediately threw the cigarette away, and from that day she had no appetite for smoking.

Rosa explained that during one of our witnessing sessions, she had asked me about this smoking habit, and remembered that I had told her not to worry about bad habits: "Jesus will take care of them." Also she then realised that although there is no scripture stating that Christians cannot smoke, the Bible does say that our body is the temple of God, and basically, we should protect this marvellous body and that this is another way of honouring God.

This change for Rosa was instant, and it does happen for some people, but remember change is also gradual.

Victory over weakness

Some years ago, I met a young lady on holiday, whom I will refer to as *(Miss Saved)*, who testified that God truly saved her and changed a particular attitude she had for years.

She explained that she used to be very flirtatious for fun, and although she was married, she found it difficult to resist the urge, because she had control and enjoyed the feeling of being noticed. Miss Saved said she felt that women had this amazing ability to command attention, and that she liked to explore this power, it was like a challenge to her. A couple of her unmarried female friends would get really annoyed as she was not single, yet when they were all out together, and there was a handsome man about, she always got the attention. She said that it was not because she was better looking, "quite the opposite" she said, but somehow she knew how to play with the chemistry attraction.

One day Jesus entered her heart and she was saved, however, she was fearful that being a young inexperienced Christian, the devil would use her flirtatious attitude to set her back, because the target of her weakness was always in her face, wherever she went.

Miss Saved said she surrendered completely to God, and His grace, has kept her steadfast. She said since taking her issue to Christ, she has never had the urge to flirt. She said it does not matter how gorgeous the man is, the steadfastness of serving God made her realise that she has a more gorgeous one at home!

Miss Saved has been an inspiration to many women of faith; she continues to be a strong woman of God, who testifies that Jesus can help you overcome your weaknesses victoriously.

A direct call to attend corporate worship

This testimony is one very close to my heart as it is my cousin's experience, and it is a wonderful confirmation that we glorify God when we come together as fellow-worshippers.

Maxine said she did not feel she needed to attend church, so decided to stay in her room where she would pray and read the Bible. One day she was in bed, when she heard quite audibly, "How can you say you dine at my table, if you have not come to my house?" She looked around and was slightly confused as she was alone. She was asked the question again, then realised it must be God telling her that she needed to attend and be a member of church.

One night Maxine had a dream that she went into a church and at the front, facing the congregation, was a large Bible, which was moving around in a circular motion. When she awoke, she decided it was time to find a church. One day she was passing a Baptist church in East London and decided to go inside. She was amazed to see the same Bible she had previously dreamed about right there at the altar.

Maxine became an active member of the church. She ministered in the women's department; she was instrumental in the development of a choir and has been instrumental in bringing others to the Lord.

The Word of God Is a Defence

This victorious testimony is the experience of a lady I met whilst working in 1999. She is of Asian ethnicity but was baptised to Christ at the local Baptist Church in North London. The testimony is confirmation that reading and knowing the Bible can literally save your life as well as supernaturally. I choose to call her Miss Delivered.

Miss Delivered worked in a local factory and often used a shortcut to visit her sister. Miss Delivered's sister often told her not to walk too late through a particular alleyway, which was close to her home. She explained to Miss Delivered that although the Bible says in Psalms 23 that even if we walk through the valley of the shadow of death, we should fear no evil, God still expect us to use Heavenly wisdom and make sensible decisions.

One night Miss Delivered decided to walk through the alleyway, when she was jumped on by an assailant. The attacker held her by the throat, and during the struggle, she began to scream out and quote scriptures of protection from the Holy Bible. Neighbours heard the loud shouts, at which point her attacker fled and she was unharmed.

The Sword of the Spirit is the Word of God and, getting to know the Bible is a weapon to be used in all challenging situations.

God Hears and Responds

A relative of mine, Murleen, lived in North London with her parents. The year was 1973; Murleen was about fifteen years old and attended church regularly with her family. She told me that something amazing happened one day during prayers.

Murleen's mother was going to the local market, and had asked her to hang out the washing, whilst she was out. Murleen said she delayed in doing her chores and did not realise time had flown by so quickly, when suddenly she heard keys in the door, it dawned on her that her mum had returned and she had not even started her chores. Murleen's mother commented that the washing was not put out to dry, and then she began to hang them herself.

Murleen said she felt sorry for being unhelpful. She knelt down to pray in her bedroom, and whilst doing that, she opened her Bible and placed it on the bed directly in front of her. Murleen's Bible was a standard size Bible suitable for early teens; the written word was quite close, which made the actual book quite compact. She prayed that Jesus would make her a more obedient person, and when she opened her eyes, she saw that a section of the scriptures had cleared away in a circle shape with light around the border. In the middle were the words: "Take heed though foolish heart." Murleen stared at the sight until the words of the pages came back together. She explained that the feeling of wonder and awe rushed through her mind at the thought that God spoke to her. She was not worried, rather she thought of how God spoke to Moses and other great prophets in the Bible. Murleen said from that moment, she became mindful to do things that would be pleasing to God.

Murleen's testimony is awesome; reading the Bible educates you to the knowledge of Christ. It keeps you connected to God with the many examples and instructions He has placed in the text, and the Bible is also a way that God speaks to His people.

Divine Fasting Instruction

From 1982 to 1997 I was a Sales Manager for a large education company. I travelled extensively, attended international conferences, dined and slept in exquisite hotels. I was good at my work and managed a large team of representatives who were absolutely fabulous people. I was always praying through the years, but work and family was my priority. Then one day, I became unwell.

I had sciatica and became inactive for months. When I eventually returned to work, I was not getting any results, which was devastating as I was on a performance related pay contract.

I was at home one afternoon. I recall washing the dishes and reflecting on my situation, when suddenly, I had this urge to sing praises then something very interesting happened. I felt very light-weight so I proceeded to kneel down to pray; however, I lay down on the floor instead, literally across the doorway of the kitchen. If anyone had seen me, the top half of my body was in the hall and the other half in the kitchen. In that position, I began to pray, when suddenly a voice spoke, I don't remember if it was audible or if it came from within me, however, the voice said: "You need to fast for three days." I was not used to fasting, but this was so profound that I decided to fast as instructed.

The next day I was given an assignment on a promotion the company was conducting. I was determined to fast and whenever I was offered food, I politely refused and prayed for strength. The first day was dreadful, the second day was more manageable, but still I got no sales.

On the third day of my fasting, I went through the same temptation of food being offered to me, so I continued to pray at intervals. The day went slowly and then just before we decided to close the exhibition, I saw a tall gentleman walking towards the stand with two children. He came over to me and I began to demonstrate the educational products to the family. He decided to purchase everything I had shown him. Before signing the form, he hesitated and looked up, quite puzzled, so I asked him if he had any more questions. He replied that he could not believe he was signing the purchase agreement because usually he would think about it for a few weeks. I smiled, because I knew it was Divine favour. After that day, I was successful at every exhibition I worked. The Lord knew that I needed to be recharged so I thank God that He is always there for us. He told Joshua of the Old Testament that he should meditate upon the Holy Scriptures day and night; the Lord told Joshua that he should only be courageous and he will have great success (Joshua 1:8).

Immediate Supernatural Answer

I believe Jesus' word when He said "ask and it shall be given" and so when I am in the inner courts of prayer, I have asked God about events that I have read in His Word. One most memorable question I asked God whilst praying was about the three Hebrew boys in the fire furnace, I was overwhelmed by their experience and wanted to know more about it.

When I entered into prayer, I got to the stage where I was in the inner courts. I heard softly "Ask". I asked about the Hebrew boys being in the extreme heat. I was blown over because spoken directly to my spirt, was, "I changed the temperature." I became so excited that I just kept crying and praising God.

I encourage you in your walk with Christ to keep asking questions, and direct as many of your questions to Jesus. Asking God questions will strengthen your ability to communicate with the Lord effectively; remember prayer should be a conversation, and a part of talking to Jesus is that you need to wait for His response.

You'll be fine!

About the Author

Angela Briscoe is Reverend at Jesus Is Ministries (JI) the Enfield branch of Bibleway Churches UK. Jamaican by birth, she is one of four children born in Jamaica. Angela's mother and father moved to England, leaving her and three other siblings two with their maternal grandparents and two with their paternal grandparents. Her parents worked hard and secured a home in North London and the family were reunited when Angela was eight years old.

Angela obeyed the call of God in 2008 to start Jesus Is Ministries (JI) in Enfield Middlesex and since then, has strived to be effective and relevant for Christ in her community.

With a passion for empowering new converts, she constantly seeks to learn and impart her learning to anyone she comes in contact with as well as the congregation she serves.

Lightning Source UK Ltd.
Milton Keynes UK
UKOW07f0804060515

250963UK00008B/25/P